ANCIENT MEDICINE

Andrew Langley

Raintree

Chicago, Illinois

EXPRESS EDITION

www.capstonepul
Visit our website to find out
more information about
Heinemann-Raintree books.

☎ Phone 888-454-2279
🖱 Visit www.capstonepub.com
   to browse our catalog and order online.

Edited by Andrew Farrow, Adam Miller, and
  Vaarunika Dharmapala
Designed by Philippa Jenkins
Original illustrations © Capstone Global Library
  Ltd 2013
Illustrations by Oxford Designers & Illustrators
Picture research by Ruth Blair

Originated by Capstone Global Library Ltd
Printed and bound in China by Leo Paper
  Products Ltd

16 15 14 13 12
10 9 8 7 6 5 4 3 2 1

**Library of Congress Cataloging-in-Publication
Data**
Langley, Andrew, 1949-
  Ancient medicine / Andrew Langley.
    p. cm. — (Medicine through the ages)
  Includes bibliographical references and index.
  ISBN 978-1-4109-4660-7 (hb) (freestyle express)) —
  ISBN 978-1-4109-4666-9 (pb) (freestyle express)) 1.
Medicine, Ancient. 2. Medicine — History. I. Title.
  R135.L36 2013b
  610.938 — dc23   2012001299

Acknowledgments
We would like to thank the following for
permission to reproduce photographs: Alamy
pp. 17 (© Hemis), 18 (© Prisma Bildagentur AG);
Getty Images pp. 6 (Jane Sweeney/Robert Harding),
7 (SSPL), 9, 10, 13 (The Bridgeman Art Library),
20 (AFP), 28 (Hulton Archive), 29 (DEA/G.
Dagli Orti), 39 (Danita Delimont/Gallo Images);
Photolibrary pp. 15 (Still Pictures), 24 (Norbert
Reismann/Doc-Stock), 27 (Leonardo Diaz Romero/
Age Fotostock), 30 (Robert Harding Travel), 38
(Photoservice Electa), 40 (Imagebroker RF/Guenter
Fischer); Science Photo Library pp. 16 (Mark
De Fraeye), 34 (Sheila Terry); Shutterstock pp. 5 (
© Stuart Elflett), 8 (© Efremova Irina); Topfoto p. 12
(Charles Walker); Wellcome Library pp.14, 19 (Mark
de Fraeye); Wellcome Library, London pp. 11, 21, 22,
23, 25, 26, 31, 32, 33, 35, 36, 37.

Cover photograph of a Pompeiian fresco
showing the battle wounds of Aeneas, from
the Archaeological Museum of Naples, Italy,
reproduced with permission of Science Photo
Library (Sheila Terry).

Every effort has been made to contact copyright
holders of any material reproduced in this book. Any
omissions will be rectified in subsequent printings if
notice is given to the publisher.

Contents

Some words are shown in bold, **like this**. You can find out what they mean by looking in the glossary. You can also look out for them in the "Word Station" box at the bottom of each page.

The Beginnings of Medicine

The ways people treat and prevent illness are known as **medicine**. People have always needed medicine in their lives.

The earliest human beings lived about 2 million years ago. As they moved around looking for food and shelter, they would have gotten hurt or sick. So they developed ways to treat these problems.

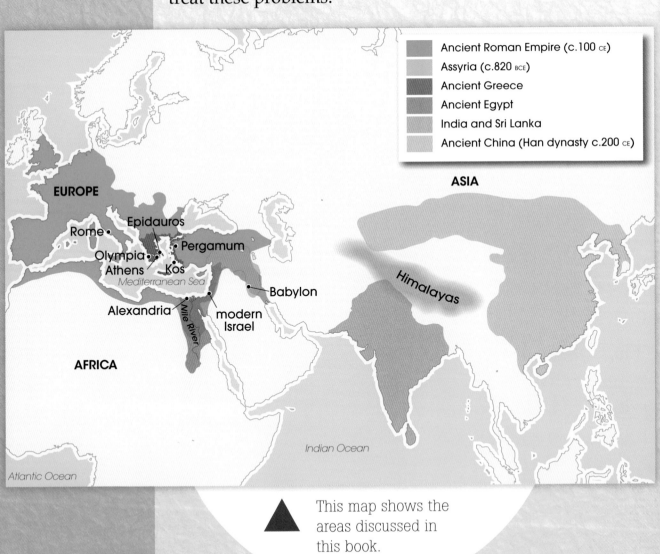

Ancient Roman Empire (c.100 CE)
Assyria (c.820 BCE)
Ancient Greece
Ancient Egypt
India and Sri Lanka
Ancient China (Han dynasty c.200 CE)

EUROPE

ASIA

Rome · Epidauros · Pergamum
Olympia
Athens · Kos
Mediterranean Sea
Alexandria · Babylon
modern Israel
Nile River
Himalayas

AFRICA

Indian Ocean

Atlantic Ocean

This map shows the areas discussed in this book.

Insects such as flies and mosquitoes can carry disease to humans.

Hunters and gatherers

Yet these first humans did not suffer from many deadly **diseases**. Diseases are health problems that prevent the body from working correctly.

This may be because they lived in small groups and constantly moved around. This made it less likely for **infections** to pass from person to person. An infection is when a tiny living thing enters the body and makes a person sick.

The rise of disease

By about 8000 BCE, many people began to develop **settlements**. Settlements are places where groups of people settle down to live. People grew plants for food. They also kept animals that provided meat and milk.

Because people stayed together in one place, it was easier to catch infections. Cows and other animals also carried diseases. So did rats and insects. Disease became a problem.

Medicine and magic

These early people did not know what caused deadly **diseases**. If the sickness had no obvious cause, they believed it was sent by gods or spirits.

So each group had a **shaman**. This person was both a religious leader and a doctor. It was believed that the shaman could draw on the gods' power. He could use this power to **cure** sick people, or make them healthy again.

This modern-day shaman lives in the country of South Africa.

MAGICAL MEDICINE TODAY

There are shamans in several places today. Some are in Africa, South Korea, and Japan. They are believed to communicate with the spirit world. They perform special ceremonies to cure sickness.

This human skull dates from 2200–2000 BCE. You can see that trepanning was used on it. Three holes are visible.

Plants and holes in the head

People also figured out more natural ways to treat illnesses. A broken bone might be protected by coating it in mud and drying it in the sun. Local plants were used to stop pain or to help cuts heal.

Trepanning involved cutting a hole in the skull. It may have helped with headaches. Trepanning was an early form of **surgery**. Surgery is the treatment of an **injury** (harm to the body) or disease with an operation.

How do we know about early humans?

There are no written records of early humans. But scientists can study skeletons and other remains of bodies. These show how ancient people might have been affected by disease or injury. Cave paintings and objects such as tools also give us clues about their lives.

Egypt and the Middle East

By about 3000 BCE, some farming **settlements** grew. They became the world's first **civilizations**. Civilizations are large, well-organized groups of people. One of the greatest civilizations was ancient Egypt. It was in northeast Africa (see the map on page 4).

In ancient Egypt, crops grew well along the Nile River. As a result, many people chose to settle along this river.

As towns grew in Egypt, more people lived close to each other. They also lived closer to animals. It was easy for **infections** to spread. Travelers and soldiers also carried infections from one place to another.

Epidemics

Civilizations began to experience the first **epidemics**. Epidemics are when **diseases** spread very quickly. Deadly diseases such as **smallpox** spread through crowded areas. Smallpox causes blisters (sores). Many people died as a result of epidemics. The ancient Egyptians had no effective **medicine** to fight these diseases.

Desert and river dangers

The ancient Egyptians also suffered from illnesses caused by their surroundings. People breathed in sand from the nearby desert areas. This made them sick. Others were attacked by worms that lived in the mud of the Nile River. The worms entered a person's body and damaged **organs** such as the heart.

This Egyptian painting shows people preparing for a funeral. A stone coffin is in the middle. It is a container for a dead body.

MUMMIES AND MEDICINE

The ancient Egyptians believed a person's body should be saved after death. They developed a way to dry out the body, so it would not rot. They removed the heart and other organs inside the body. Then they dried the skin with salts and wrapped it in cloth. This made a "mummy." Today, scientists use these mummies to study the diseases of ancient Egypt.

Sorcerers and surgeons

The **civilization** of ancient Egypt lasted for over 2,000 years. During that time, the Egyptians learned a lot about **medicine**.

Egyptians believed that most illnesses were caused by evil spirits. So the earliest doctors were also priests or people believed to have magic powers. They cast spells or gave patients special charms (jewelry) to wear. They also used special creams to scare off evil spirits.

The first doctors

Over time, doctors learned that some treatments worked better than others. To **cure** many **diseases**, they used natural substances. They used **minerals** (for example, coal). They also used parts of plants and animals.

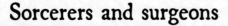

A man named Imhotep (shown in this statue) was a famous doctor in Egypt.

Doctors learned to clean wounds with special mixtures. They then wrapped the wounds with bandages made of a cloth called **linen**. Doctors stitched together serious cuts with copper needles. To heal broken bones, doctors made **casts** (protective coverings). They use cows' milk and other materials.

Precious papyrus

Several "textbooks" from ancient Egypt help teach us about Egyptian medicine. These are written on rolls of **papyrus**. This is a kind of paper made from water plants. These writings list recipes for medicines. They also list instructions for treating **injuries**.

Did the Egyptians cut up bodies?

Ancient Egyptian**s** prepared dead bodies for burial by removing **organs** from inside the body (see page 9). But this did not mean they took out the organs to study them. In fact, many experts think it was forbidden to **dissect** bodies in ancient Egypt. Dissecting is cutting apart a body for study.

This shows an important Egyptian writing known as the Edwin Smith papyrus. It lists details of over 40 injuries and how to treat them.

Medical advances in Mesopotamia

Egypt was not the only ancient **civilization** in the area. From about 3500 BCE, several great kingdoms developed in a place called Mesopotamia. Today, this is part of the country called Iraq. The people who lived in Mesopotamia made early discoveries in **medicine**.

King Hammurabi led the kingdom of Babylon (see the map on page 4). About 1780 BCE, he had the Code of Laws carved onto a **pillar**. A pillar is a tall, thin structure often used to hold up a building. The laws included rules for doctors.

Other records come from about 660 BCE in the Assyrian kingdom (see the map on page 4). They were scratched on clay writing tablets (small, flat pieces of clay). Many of these tablets tell how to **diagnose** (study and identify) and **cure** common illnesses.

This carving on the pillar of Hammurabi shows the king of Babylon (left). He is being given the Code of Laws by a god.

Hebrew healers

The Hebrews founded a civilization in about 1020 BCE. It was in what is now the country of Israel (see the map on page 4). They believed that **disease** was sent from God as punishment for wrongdoing. But the Hebrews also developed practical ways to treat diseases.

Their main weapon was **hygiene**, or keeping clean. By keeping clothes, bodies, and homes clean, they lessened the chance of **infection**.

Quarantine

The Hebrews invented the process of **quarantine**. This means that sick patients are kept apart from other people, so they cannot pass on their illness.

This sculpture shows a god holding a nail. It is from ancient Mesopamia. The belief in gods was still a large part of medicine.

▶

THE FIRST WOMEN DOCTORS

One of the earliest known female doctors was Peseshet. She was described as "head of lady physicians [doctors]" and probably lived about 2500 BCE. Some women also worked as doctors and **midwives** in ancient Mesopotamia. Midwives are nurses who help women with childbirth.

India

About 1500 BCE, people from Central Asia began settling in India (see the map on page 4). By 500 BCE, they had built a strong **civilization** in northern India. They developed their own language, called **Sanskrit**. They created their own religion, or set of beliefs in gods. It was called **Hinduism**.

Ayurvedic medicine

These early Indians also created their own kind of **medicine**. The main system of treatment was called **Ayurveda**. It was based on the **Vedas**. These are holy books that helped form the ideas of the religion Hinduism.

Dhanvantari is an important figure in Hinduism. He is doctor to the gods. He is also the god of Ayurvedic medicine. This statue stands outside a hospital in Mumbai, India.

WORD STATION
Hinduism religion developed in ancient India, based on writings such as the Vedas

Keeping clean by bathing in important rivers is a part of Hinduism.

COMMON CONFUSIONS

Ayurvedic medicine today

Ayurvedic medicine is still practiced across India, Asia, Europe, and the United States. But it is not the same as the ancient Ayurveda. Instead of only using plants to make medicines, most Ayurvedic doctors today also use modern medicines.

Ayurvedic practices

Ayurvedic medicine recommended ways to stay healthy. It also recommended **cures**. Doctors stressed the importance of **hygiene**. They also recommended a good diet and regular exercise. These are important parts of Hinduism.

Ayurvedic doctors believed that bodies contain certain amounts of important substances. These include blood and wind. They thought that illness was caused when the balance between these substances was disturbed.

Doctors also identified 107 points on the human body. The points could be massaged (gently rubbed) to allow healing. It was believed that an **injury** at any of these points could be deadly.

How do we know about ancient Indian medicine?

Ayurvedic medicine was based on the **Vedas**. Two other early writings describe medicine in ancient India. The first deals mainly with observing and **diagnosing** over 200 kinds of sickness. The second contains a large section on **surgery**. Both texts give recipes for many kinds of medicine. The ingredients include gold, special plants called **herbs**, and more.

Developing surgery

The ancient Indians were the first people to make major discoveries in surgery. Indian **surgeons** (doctors who perform surgery) could remove painful objects called **kidney stones**. They had over 120 different **instruments** (tools) for this and other tasks.

Many Ayurvedic medicines are still prepared the way they were in ancient times. Here herbs are being prepared for use.

Herbs and spices are crushed together here to make medicine.

In his writings, a doctor named Susruta explained how to perform a kind of surgery. He told how flaps of skin from one part of the body can be moved and sewn to cover a problem in another part. Doctors use similar steps today.

The ashtangas

Ayurvedic doctors divided medicine into *ashtangas*, or parts:

- internal medicine (inside the body)
- childbirth and **diseases** of children
- surgery
- treatment of the head region (eyes, ears, nose, and throat)
- preventing **infectious** diseases (diseases that spread)
- possession by evil spirits (an early kind of **psychiatry**, the study of diseases of the mind)
- the **curing** of poisons, and removing poisons from the body
- love potions (to help couples have children).

Treating problems of the mind

Indian doctors helped develop **psychiatry**. This is the study of **diseases** of the mind. They thought that the mind contained certain important parts. **Mental** problems (problems of the mind) were caused when these parts were not in balance.

Some doctors believed that invisible spirits caused mental problems. Others blamed tiny living things in the air. The main treatment involved burning special **herbs** to clean the air.

Diseases in children

Evil spirits were blamed for causing many illnesses in children. **Ayurvedic** doctors treated these problems with **chants** and herbs. Chants are holy words or groups of words repeated many times. Herbs were once again burned to clean the air.

Ayurvedic medicine uses chants to help healing. These words were sometimes carved on stones, to help with prayer.

WORD STATION
mental relating to the mind

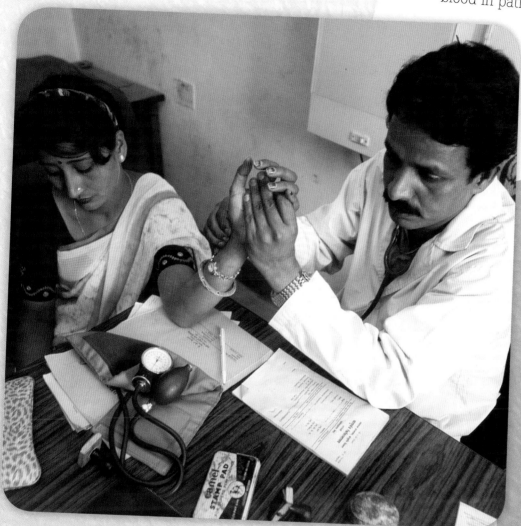

Ayurvedic doctors check the flow of blood in patients.

Channels of the body

Ayurvedic **medicine** often focuses on the different "channels" in the body. These channels carry food, water, blood, and more to where they are needed. Ayurvedic doctors believed that disease occurs when these channels get damaged or blocked. They had several ways to open the channels up again. Among these were massages and steam baths.

China

China began as many separate states, or areas. In 221 BCE, these states were brought together under one leader (see the map on page 4). During this period, the country developed very quickly.

Early discoveries

Studying **medicine** became a respected job in China. It became separate from religion. The early Chinese made many important discoveries about how the human body works. They also learned how **disease** and **injury** can be treated.

Many parts of ancient Chinese medicine are still used in China today. These people are having **herbs** applied to special points on their bodies.

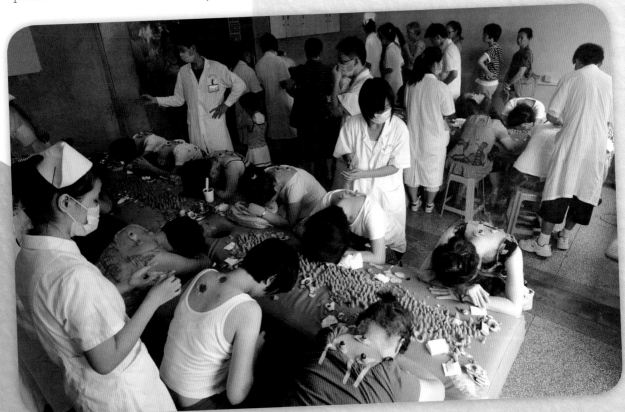

This illustration appeared in a Chinese book from 1439. It shows a man teaching students about medicine.

Have there been any advances in Chinese medicine?

Doctors in China have respect for tradition. They have followed teachings and writings that are over 2,000 years old. In the last 100 years, though, some new ideas from other countries have been used as well.

The body in balance

The ancient Chinese believed that all the parts of the human body must be kept in balance. They believed that the body was made up of fire, water, earth, wood, and metal. Doctors aimed to **cure** disease by balancing these parts inside the patient.

The Chinese also believed that the world was ruled by a pair of opposite forces, or sources of activity. They were called **yin and yang**. Chinese doctors thought there was a constant struggle in the body between yin and yang. For instance, if a person was very angry, then yang was gaining control. The doctor's job was to return yin and yang to their proper balance.

Diagnosis and treatment

Chinese doctors were trained to look at a patient very closely. They also took the patient's **pulse**. The pulse is the repeated beating of **arteries** as blood pushes through them. (Arteries are tubes in the body that carry blood away from the heart.)

All of this gave the doctor a detailed picture of how the energy forces were flowing through the body. These energy forces were called *chi*. These tests showed imbalances between **yin and yang**.

Chinese doctors had thousands of pills, powders, and drinks to give patients. Many were meant to control the flow of *chi*.

Chinese doctors measured the pulse at different points on the patient's body, including the wrist.

WORD STATION
pulse repeated beating of arteries as blood pushes through them

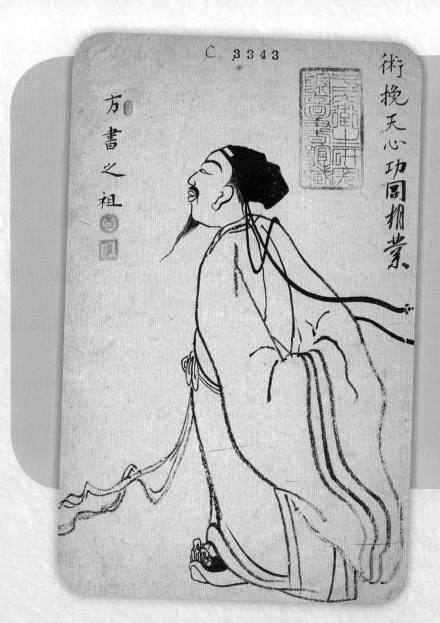

C. 3343

方書之祖

術挽天心功同相業

ZHANG ZHONGJING
Chinese doctor
(c. 150–219 CE)

Zhang Zhongjing was born in China. We know very little about his life. But several of his texts have survived. The most famous of these is called *On Cold Damage*. It explains ways to treat some of the **infectious diseases** that were spreading in China at the time.

The Yellow Emperor's Book

The earliest writings about Chinese **medicine** are in *The Yellow Emperor's Book*. This was written about 200 BCE. The text discusses how to be healthy in a natural way. It looks at the meaning of the life forces of yin and yang. It also examines **acupuncture** (see pages 24 and 25). This book was the basis of all early Chinese medicine. It is still admired today.

Getting the needle

Acupuncture has been used for over 2,000 years in China. Thin needles are pushed into the skin. Then they are turned or moved back and forth. These needles were first made of bone or stone. Later, they were made of metal.

The Chinese believed that *chi* flows through a person along special "channels." By inserting needles at special points on the body, the doctor could affect the balance of *chi*. One of the most popular uses of acupuncture was to relieve pain.

Another way to control the flow of *chi* was by burning tiny balls of **herbs** at special points on the body. Doctors thought the heat from the burning warmed the body's channels. This would make them work better.

MEDICINAL HERBS IN CHINA

In a Chinese book from about 50 CE, over 300 herbs were listed that could treat illness. They included cinnamon, ginger, and licorice. These herbs are still very popular in Chinese medicine today.

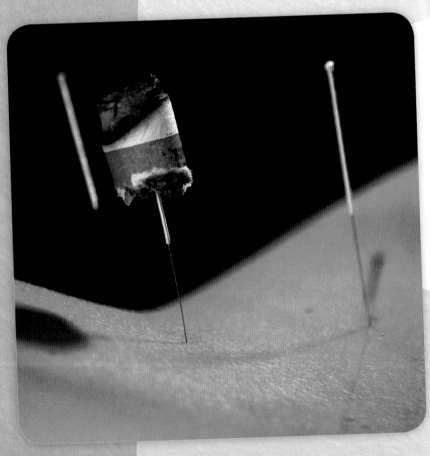

An herb called moxa is burning on the end of a needle. The needle has been placed at a special point on the body.

WORD STATION

acupuncture Chinese treatment in which thin needles are inserted at special points on the bod

What have we learned from Chinese medicine?

Ancient Chinese ideas about the balance of forces in the body have not become part of modern **medicine** in the West.

But some treatments, such as acupuncture, are still used today. Chinese doctors also made several important discoveries about medicine. Here are two of them:

- The Chinese knew that blood was pumped through the body by the heart. This was not known in Europe until about 1550 CE. ("CE" refers to the time after the Christian religion began.)

- The Chinese knew that people need to eat healthy substances called **vitamins**, or their health would suffer. They knew this over 1,700 years ago.

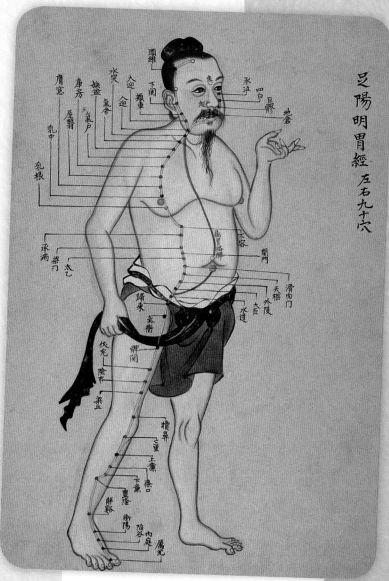

▲ This chart shows the acupuncture points on the body.

Greece

Greek **civilization** developed from about 800 BCE. At first, there was no central ruler. People lived in separate areas called city-states. Even so, the Greeks saw themselves as held together by common beliefs and discoveries. Over time, Greek influence spread widely around the Mediterranean Sea (see the map on page 4).

This modern artwork shows a patient visiting the ancient Greek temple of Epidauros. His leg is being licked by a snake (see page 27).

Illness and the gods

The Greeks told stories about gods and goddesses. One story said that the goddess Pandora opened a forbidden jar or box. This released all kinds of evil into the world—including **diseases**. The Greeks believed that sickness and **injury** were caused by the gods.

Temple treatments

People linked certain gods with healing powers. The best-known Greek god of healing was Asklepios.

Religious buildings, called temples, were built all over the Greek world for the worship of Asklepios. The biggest was at Epidauros, in southern Greece. Thousands of people came there every year to pray for **cures** for diseases.

THE SNAKES OF ASKLEPIOS

The ancient Greeks connected snakes with Asklepios. A snake was kept at Epidauros. Snakes were even used to lick a sick person's body. The symbol of healing was a rod with a snake curled around it.

Statues of Asklepios, such as this one, were always shown with a rod and a snake.

The early Greeks and health

In ancient Greece, men spent a lot of time training in sports and other activities. They felt it was important to be fit and healthy. Women did not take part in these activities. This was because they were not supposed to appear in public.

Many early Greek doctors specialized in fitness. Others dealt with the **injuries** suffered by soldiers. Wounds were cleaned with wine or a sour substance called vinegar. They were then treated with **herbs**. Finally, they were tied up tightly, to stop the bleeding.

These men appear on a Greek vase from the 400s BCE. The scene shows athletes training for the Olympic Games.

This marble carving shows a Greek doctor treating a patient.

Natural causes of disease

Over time, Greek people explored the idea that **diseases** were brought about by natural causes, not the gods. They believed that the body contained four important substances called **humors**. These humors were thought to control a person's health and the way he or she acts.

In about 470 BCE, a man named Alcmaeon argued that humans experience feelings through the brain. A man named Democritus stated that babies are created by the mixing of "seeds" from both parents. We now know that these ideas were correct.

THE GREAT PLAGUE OF ATHENS

In 430 BCE, the people of Athens, Greece, were struck by a deadly **infectious** disease. It happened again three years later. The disease caused vomiting (throwing up), bleeding, and blindness. It spread quickly. Many thousands of people died. Even today, experts are not sure what kind of disease this was.

The mystery of Hippocrates

A man named Hippocrates was the most famous of all ancient Greek doctors. Very little is known about Hippocrates' life. Experts think he was born about 460 BCE.

But his work helped to separate **medicine** from religion. Medicine came to be seen as a job. Doctors around the world today still take the **Hippocratic Oath** (see the box below).

The Hippocratic Oath

For over 2,000 years, students studying medicine have made the Hippocratic Oath when they become doctors.

Among the promises they make are:

- to use their power to help the sick, and never to do harm
- never to give a patient a deadly poison, even if asked
- not to cut open the body (which is the work of **surgeons**)
- never to have sexual contact with patients
- to keep secret anything they are told by a patient.

This tiled floor shows Hippocrates inviting Asklepios to study medicine.

Hippocrates advised doctors to carefully examine each patient. This carving shows the god Asklepios on the right.

The Hippocratic writings

There is an important collection of writings about ancient Greek medicine called the Hippocratic writings. Nobody knows for sure whether Hippocrates actually wrote any of them. These writings include stories of patients and **epidemics**. There are also notes on dealing with specific problems and **diseases**.

The most important development of the time was **diagnosing** illness. The Hippocratic writings reflect this. They advise doctors to observe a patient's **symptoms** (signs of disease) very carefully. Eyes, skin, temperature, and more should be studied. Doctors should listen closely to any noises inside the body.

The work of Aristotle

Long after Hippocrates, other Greeks pushed forward new ideas about **medicine**. The greatest of these was Aristotle, who lived from 384 to 322 BCE. He studied the world around him, including how the body and mind worked.

Aristotle watched **embryos** (newly formed chicks) developing in hens' eggs. Based on these observations, he decided that the heart was the center of all life.

Aristotle also **dissected** the bodies of animals. This allowed him to look at the **organs** and more inside.

Aristotle was the son of a doctor. He studied many different kinds of science.

This artwork shows the ancient Greeks Herophilus (left) and Erasistratus (right).

Medicine in Alexandria

Aristotle taught a prince. The prince went on to be Alexander the Great, an important leader. In 331 BCE, Alexander founded the Egyptian city of Alexandria. It was an important place for medicine.

In Alexandria around 300 BCE, a scientist named Herophilus learned about body parts. He noted that some body parts carry out **digestion** (breaking down and using food). Others carry out **reproduction** (having young). He also learned about the brain.

At about the same time, a man named Erasistratus was studying the heart. By dissecting it, he found it contained four one-way valves, or flaps.

These discoveries were possible because rulers allowed scientists to dissect human bodies. After about 250 BCE, this stopped. Nobody knows why. People would not dissect bodies again until over 1,500 years later, in Europe.

Rome

As the Greek **civilization** grew weaker, Rome became the greatest power in the Mediterranean Sea. By about 100 BCE, the Romans had control of a large area of land (see the map on page 4).

Early Roman medicine

At first, the Romans had few doctors. They believed people were responsible for keeping themselves healthy. The early Romans also used treatments based on religion and magic. For example, some believed that a head cold would disappear if the sufferer kissed a mule on the nose!

This Roman painting shows a soldier wounded in battle. A doctor is trying to remove an arrowhead from the soldier's thigh, using a special tool.

▶

Greek thinkers influenced Roman medicine. This picture shows the great Greeks thinkers Plato, Anaxagoras, and Democritus.

The Greeks in Rome

The Romans' practical knowledge of **medicine** came from Greece and Egypt. An important Greek **surgeon** named Asclepiades came to Italy about 100 BCE.

Asclepiades believed that the body depended on the correct arrangement of tiny substances. He called these tiny bits "atoms." If these were blocked, the person became sick. Asclepiades treated illness with gentle exercise, bathing, and massage. He also recommended drinking wine.

Galen

The best-known expert about **medicine** in ancient Rome was Galen. He was a Greek who lived from 129 to 216 CE. He worked in Rome for much of his life. Galen became famous for **dissecting** animals in front of audiences. Some of the animals were still alive.

The influence of Galen

Galen is thought to have written about 350 books. We can still read many of these today. His texts contained many new ideas about how the body worked. For example, he discovered that the **arteries** contain blood. People had previously thought only **veins** (tubes in the body) carried blood.

Galen was born in what is now the country of Turkey. His family was wealthy, so he was able to visit famous teachers.

WORD STATION
vein special type of tube in the body that carries blood

This stone carving shows a midwife helping a woman give birth.

Galen's ideas about the human body and the treatment of **disease** were followed for hundreds of years. However, many of his ideas were later proven to be wrong. For example, his belief that blood was made in the **organ** called the **liver** was a mistake. It is actually made in the bones. He also thought that **bloodletting** (the cutting of veins to release blood) was the best way to treat many diseases. In fact, it left the patient weaker.

FEMALE DOCTORS

Throughout the time of the Romans, women as well as men worked as doctors. They were possibly only allowed to treat other women and children. It is also possible they focused only on female problems, such as diseases of the breast. Female **midwives** were nurses who helped mothers with childbirth.

Roman surgery

Surgeons in Rome were skilled in many kinds of **surgery**. Writings by doctors describe how to **amputate** (cut off) damaged limbs, such as legs. There are stories of operating on the skull and the eye.

The writings of a doctor named Celsus tell us what kinds of surgery were done about 30 CE. Roman surgeons developed as many as 200 different **instruments** to perform surgery.

Herbal cures and drugs

Doctors used drugs to treat **disease** and **injuries**. Many of these were made from common ingredients, such as honey and eggs. Sometimes ingredients were brought from far away, such as fruits from the country of India.

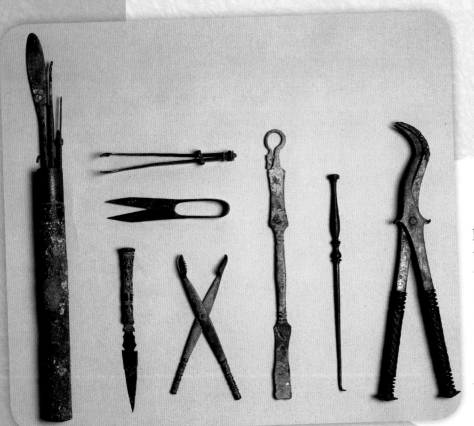

Roman doctors used a wide variety of instruments. These examples are from the 100s CE.

In this stone carving, a doctor is examining a patient with an eye injury.

Dioscorides wrote about the different ingredients used in **medicine** about 64 CE. He listed over 1,000 substances that could be used as drugs. This included plants, animal materials, and **minerals**.

TREATING MENTAL PATIENTS

In ancient Rome, people with **mental** problems were either cared for at home or left to wander the streets. Some doctors recommended **bloodletting** and drugs as treatment. Some tried calmer methods, such as massage or special diets. A few believed that people with mental problems should be treated with horrible treatments such as starving or being beaten.

Fresh water and drains

The Romans knew the importance of fresh water for public health. Dirty water can cause **disease**. Between 312 BCE and 226 CE, 11 huge **aqueducts** (special long pipes) were built to bring fresh water to the center of Rome. There were also public bathrooms and baths. Special systems were developed to carry away human waste.

The ancient world and after

In Roman times, **medicine** had come a long way since the earliest humans. The earliest people had blamed sickness on the gods. Over time, doctors had come to realize that the causes of disease were natural, and could be treated naturally. This led to many discoveries in the **civilizations** of ancient Greece and Rome.

The Roman Empire in the West was destroyed by invaders about 476 CE. For hundreds of years afterward, doctors continued using the methods passed down by Hippocrates and Galen.

The Romans built public baths in many cities. These ruins are in the modern-day country of Libya.

view from above

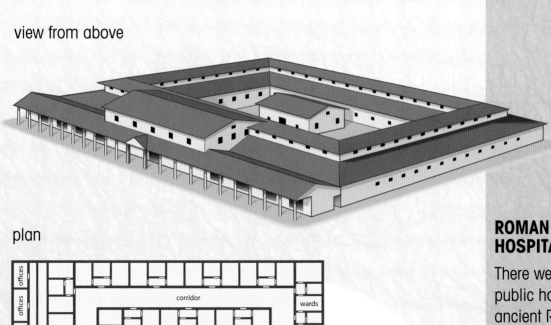

plan

offices
offices
offices

corridor

wards

wards

courtyard

entrance

treatment
room

wards

wards

offices
offices
offices

corridor

| 0 | | 5 | | 10 meters |
| 0 | 10 | 20 | 30 feet |

ROMAN HOSPITALS

There were no public hospitals in ancient Rome. The only true hospitals were for the Roman army. But these were only for sick or wounded soldiers (see the illustration at left).

This is the plan of a Roman military hospital. It had a treatment room and separate rooms, or wards, for the patients.

However, the main advances in medicine were still to come. They would come from a new civilization in a part of the world called the Middle East.

Timeline

BCE	
c. 2 million	Small groups of people wander looking for food
c. 8000	People develop the earliest human **settlements**. This encourages the spread of **disease**.
c. 3500	The earliest **civilizations** begin in Mesopotamia
c. 3000	Egypt is united under one king
c. 1780	King Hammurabi of Babylon orders his Code of Laws to be carved onto a **pillar**
c. 1600–1550	Important Egyptian writings about **medicine** are created
c. 1020	The Hebrew civilization is founded in present-day Israel
c. 800	The ancient Greek civilization is established
c. 660	King Assurbanipal of Assyria creates a library of clay tablets. These include ideas about treating illness.
c. 500	A strong civilization controls much of northern India. **Ayurvedic** medicine soon spreads there.
c. 470	Alcmaeon of Sicily says that the brain is the main **organ** of feeling
c. 460	Hippocrates is born on the island of Kos
c. 450	Empedocles of Sicily describes the four **humors** of the human body

430–426	A terrible **epidemic** spreads through Athens, Greece
331	Alexander the Great founds the city of Alexandria in Egypt. This becomes a great place for medicine.
c. 300	Herophilus and Erasistratus **dissect** human bodies
221	China is united under a single leader
c. 200	The text of *The Yellow Emperor's Book* is written
c. 100	Rome begins to win control of a large part of the world. The Greek doctor Asclepiades arrives in Rome.
CE	
c. 30	The Roman Celsus writes about medicine
c. 64	The Greek Dioscorides writes about medicine
129	Galen is born in Pergamum, in the present-day country of Turkey
476	The Roman Empire ends in the West

Glossary

acupuncture Chinese treatment in which thin needles are inserted at special points on the body

amputate cut off

aqueduct long pipe or bridge for moving water from one place to another

artery blood vessel that carries blood away from the heart

Ayurveda main system of healing in ancient India

Ayurvedic relating to Ayurveda, the main system of healing in ancient India

BCE meaning "Before the Common Era." When this appears after a date, it refers to the time before the Christian religion began. BCE dates are always counted backward.

bloodletting cutting veins to release blood

cast protective shell put over a broken bone while it heals

CE meaning "Common Era." When this appears after a date, it refers to the time after the Christian religion began.

chant holy word or group of words repeated many times

chi energy forces that some people believe flow through the body

civilization large, well-organized group of people

cure make healthy again

diagnose identify a disease or injury by studying it closely

digestion body system that breaks down and uses food

disease health problem that prevents the body from working correctly

dissect cut up a dead body in order to study it

embryo living thing in the very early stages of its development

epidemic fast spread of a disease through an area or group of people

herb type of plant that has parts that are useful for cooking and medicine

Hinduism religion developed in ancient India, based on writings such as the Vedas

Hippocratic Oath promise taken by a doctor, agreeing to follow a code of medical behavior based on the teachings of Hippocrates

humor (in ancient medicine) one of the four important substances thought to control the body

hygiene practice of maintaining health by keeping clean

infection when tiny living things enter the body and make a person sick

infectious something, such as a disease, that spreads

injury harm to the body

instrument tool

kidney stone hard object made of salts that forms in the organs called the kidneys

linen fabric made from the flax plant

liver large organ in the body that cleans the blood, among other important jobs

medicine science of treating and preventing illness. The word is also used to mean the drugs (such as pills) that people take to get well.

mental relating to the mind

midwife specially trained nurse who helps women with childbirth

mineral natural substance, such as coal

organ part of the body that has a special function, such as the heart

papyrus kind of paper made from water plants

pillar tall, thin structure often used to hold up a building

psychiatry study of diseases of the mind

pulse repeated beating of arteries as blood pushes through them

quarantine keeping sick patients apart from other people so they cannot pass on their illness

reproduction body processes that lead to having young

Sanskrit language developed in India

settlement place where a group of people settle down to live

shaman medicine man or religious man who is believed to communicate with the spirit world

smallpox disease that causes blisters on the face and often leads to death

surgeon person who performs surgery

surgery treatment of an injury or disease with an operation rather than drugs

symptom sign that shows that a person has a disease

trepanning surgery involving cutting a hole in the skull to treat an illness

Vedas holy books that helped form the ideas behind the religion of Hinduism

vein special type of tube in the body that carries blood

vitamin healthy substance found in some foods that helps the body to grow and work

yin and yang pair of opposite forces in nature that early Chinese doctors believed needed to be in balance for a person to be healthy

Find Out More

Books

Catel, Patrick. *What Did the Ancient Greeks Do for Me?* (Linking the Past and Present). Chicago: Heinemann Library, 2011.

Catel, Patrick. *What Did the Ancient Romans Do for Me?* (Linking the Past and Present). Chicago: Heinemann Library, 2011.

Elliott, James. *Outlines of Greek and Roman Medicine.* Charleston, S.C.: BiblioBazaar, 2007.

Hartman, Eve, and Wendy Meshbesher. *The Scientists Behind Medical Advances* (Sci-Hi Scientists). Chicago: Raintree, 2011.

Kelly, Kate. *Early Civilizations: Prehistoric Times to 500 CE* (History of Medicine). New York: Facts on File, 2010.

Websites

www.historyforkids.org/learn/china/science/ chinamedicine.htm
Learn more about medicine in ancient China at this website.

www.historyforkids.org/learn/india/science/medicine.htm
This website contains lots of information about medical practices in ancient India.

www.knowitall.org/kidswork/hospital/history/ancient/ index.html
This website contains a brief guide to ancient medicine.

www.yourdiscovery.com/greece/science_and_medicine/ index.shtml
This website is full of facts about ancient Greek medicine.

Places to visit

The Exploratorium, San Francisco, California
www.exploratorium.edu

The Health Museum, Houston, Texas
www.mhms.org

International Museum of Surgical Science, Chicago, Illinois
www.imss.org

Metropolitan Museum of Art, New York City
www.metmuseum.org

National Museum of Health and Medicine, Washington, D.C.
nmhm.washingtondc.museum

More topics to research

- What does a shaman actually do?

- What evidence is left that tells us about Romans baths and aqueducts?

- How widely is traditional Chinese medicine still used in modern China and other parts of the world?

- What really happened in the Great Plague of Athens, the epidemic that spread through ancient Athens (see page 29)?

- The cover of this book shows a detail of a painting from the ancient Roman city of Pompeii. The painting depicts the hero Aeneas wounded in battle, as described in the long poem the *Aeneid*. Find out more about the figures in the painting and the story behind the scene. You could also research the kinds of tools ancient Roman doctors used on battlefields.

Index